WHY DO I GROW?

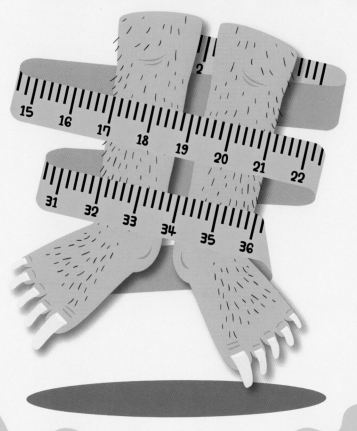

BY MADELINE TYLER

CRABTREE
PUBLISHING COMPANY
WWW.CRABTREEBOOKS.COM

Published in Canada
Crabtree Publishing
616 Welland Avenue
St. Catharines, ON
L2M 5V6

Published in the United States
Crabtree Publishing
PMB 59051
350 Fifth Ave, 59th Floor
New York, NY 10118

Published in 2019 by Crabtree Publishing Company

First Published by Book Life in 2018
Copyright © 2018 Book Life

Printed in the U.S.A./082018/CG20180601

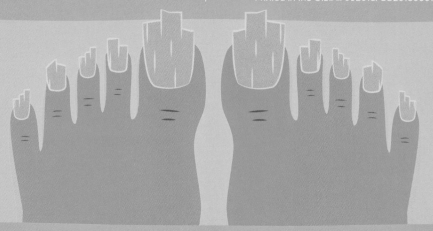

Author: Madeline Tyler

Editors: Kirsty Holmes, Kathy Middleton

Design: Danielle Rippengill

Proofreader: Janine Deschenes

Prepress technician: Samara Parent

Print coordinator: Katharine Berti

All facts, statistics, web addresses and URLs in this book were verified as valid and accurate at time of writing. No responsibility for any changes to external websites or references can be accepted by either the author or publisher.

Photographs

All images are courtesy of Shutterstock.com, unless otherwise specified. With thanks to Getty Images, Thinkstock Photo and iStockphoto. Front Cover & 1 – Dmitry Natashin, Nadzin, nasidastudio, grmarc. Images used on every spread – Nadzin, TheFarAwayKingdom. 2 – Roi and Roi. 4–7 – Iconic Bestiary. 8 – eranicle. 9 – MSSA. 10 & 11 – arborelza. 12 & 13 – Iconic Bestiary. 14 – lukpedclub. 15 – Iconic Bestiary, KIKUCHI, ByEmo, Roman Marvel. 16 – Iconic Bestiary. 17 – Ira Yapanda. 18 – Roi and Roi. 19 – LynxVector. 20 – Iconic Bestiary. 21 – svtdesign. 22 – Iconic Bestiary. 23 – user friendly, Anna Violet.

Library and Archives Canada Cataloguing in Publication

Tyler, Madeline, author.
      Why do I grow? / Madeline Tyler.

(Why do I?)
Includes index.
Issued in print and electronic formats.
ISBN 978-0-7787-5142-7 (hardcover).--
ISBN 978-0-7787-5148-9 (softcover).--
ISBN 978-1-4271-2172-1 (HTML)

      1. Human growth--Juvenile literature. 2. Human physiology--Juvenile literature. I. Title.

QP84.T95 2018   j612   C2018-902398-8
                                                        C2018-902399-6

Library of Congress Cataloging-in-Publication Data

Names: Tyler, Madeline, author.
Title: Why do I grow? / Madeline Tyler.
Description: New York, New York : Crabtree Publishing Company, 2019. |
   Series: Why do I? | Includes index.
Identifiers: LCCN 2018021331 (print) | LCCN 2018021636 (ebook) |
   ISBN 9781427121721 (Electronic) |
   ISBN 9780778751427 (hardcover) |
   ISBN 9780778751489 (pbk.)
Subjects: LCSH: Growth--Juvenile literature. | Human growth--Juvenile
   literature. | Human physiology--Juvenile literature.
Classification: LCC QH511 (ebook) | LCC QH511 .T95 2019 (print) |
   DDC 612.6--dc23
LC record available at https://lccn.loc.gov/2018021331

CONTENTS

Words that look like **this** can be found in the glossary on page 24.

How Tall Are You?

Are you taller than your friend, but shorter than your brother?

Do your fingernails always need a **trim**? Do they feel like they are not growing at all?

Has your doctor ever measured how tall you are?

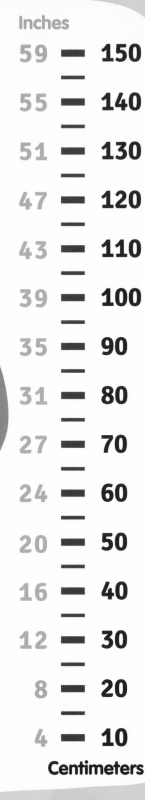

Inches

59	150
55	140
51	130
47	120
43	110
39	100
35	90
31	80
27	70
24	60
20	50
16	40
12	30
8	20
4	10

Centimeters

Children's bodies grow every day. Your bones get bigger and your bodies get taller. Some children grow quickly, and some grow slowly.

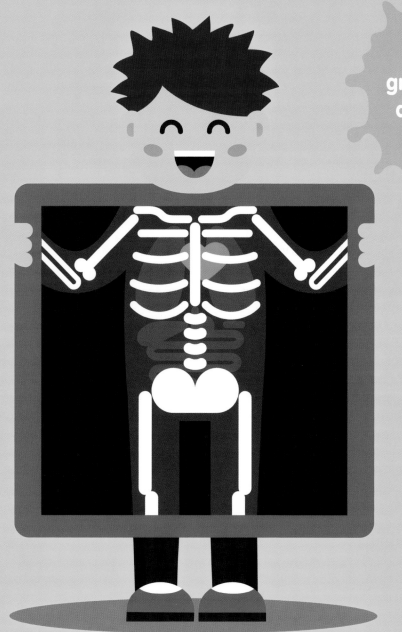

You stop growing taller as an adult.

5

Growing Up

As we get older, we grow bigger and stronger.

Growing is an important part of getting older. You might be small or short now, but one day you might be even taller than your teacher!

People usually stop growing taller when they are around 18 to 21 years old. But their hair and nails usually keep growing longer, even when they become old.

What Makes You Grow?

Your body makes **chemicals** that allow you to grow. These chemicals are called **hormones**.

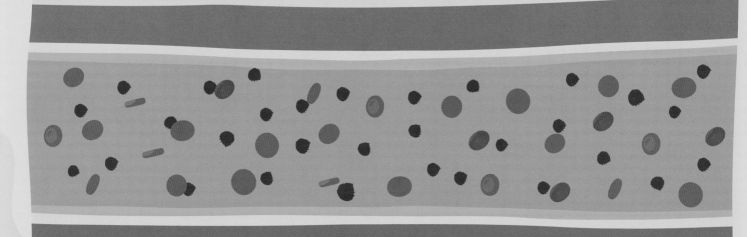

Hormones carry information and instructions that tell different parts of your body to do certain things, such as grow. Hormones are carried around your body in your blood.

Different hormones do different jobs. The main hormone that makes you grow is called growth hormone.

Hormones are made by body parts called glands.

Glands and Growth

The pituitary gland is a small gland in your brain.

The pituitary gland creates growth hormone.

There are glands in many places inside your body. The gland that helps you grow is in your brain.

A hormone made in another part of the brain gives instructions to the pituitary gland.

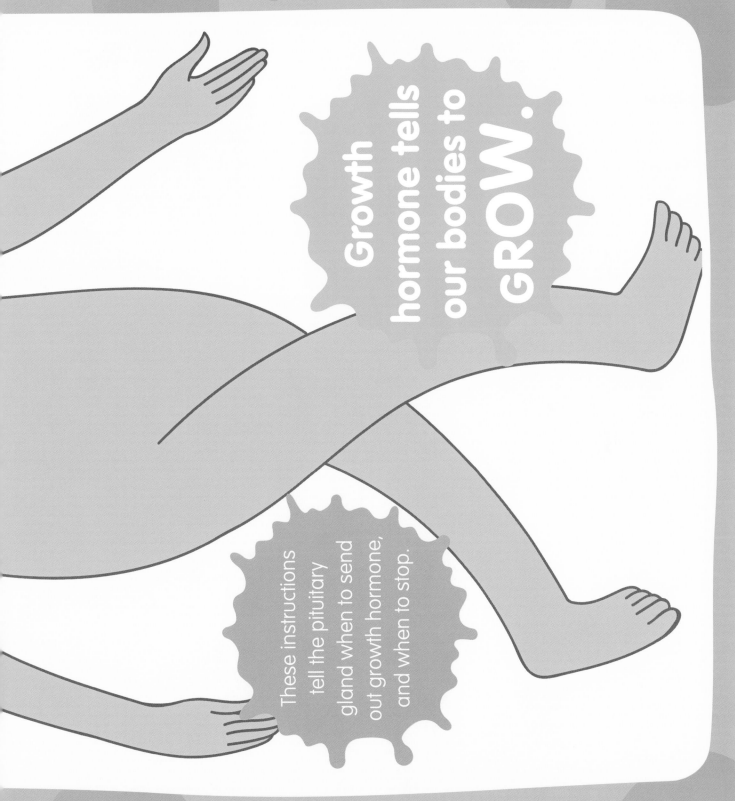

Growth hormone tells our bodies to GROW.

These instructions tell the pituitary gland when to send out growth hormone, and when to stop.

Growing Differently

Inches		Centimeters
71		180
67		170
63		160
59		150
55		140
51		130
47		120

Not everyone grows at the same **pace**. Some children might grow more quickly than other children who are the same age. Some children grow more slowly.

The children in your class might all be the same age. But are they all the same height? The hormones in each person's body decide how fast or slow they grow.

Not Just Hormones

Growth hormone is important for growing bodies, but so are a lot of other things. For children to grow strong and healthy, they also need:

- Water
- Sleep
- Exercise
- **Nutrients**

Growing is hard work. It can be very tiring. It is important to take care of your body as it is growing.

Get nutrients such as calcium from food to stay healthy.

Get the right amount of sleep. Children aged 6 to 13 need 9 to 11 hours of sleep every night.

Eat healthy food, such as fruit.

Get regular exercise.

Drink lots of water.

Growth Spurts!

Sometimes, children grow a lot in a short period of time. This is called a growth spurt and can happen at different times during their life.

A big growth spurt often happens during the preteen years, or around age 11 or 12—but the age can change from person to person!

Inches	Centimeters
55	140
51	130
47	120
43	110
8	20
4	10

During a growth spurt, the hands and feet grow first.
Teenagers often need a lot of new shoes because they
grow out of them so quickly!

Gross Growth

Toenails

Toenails grow all the time. Make sure you trim them regularly so they do not look like this!

A toenail can grow 3/4 of an inch (almost 2 cm) in a year!

Nose Hair

Everybody has hair in their nose, even babies! Your hormones change as you get older. This can make you grow bushier eyebrows and more hair in your nose—and even in your ears!

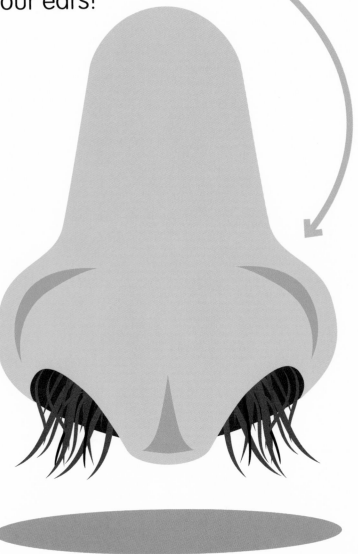

Helpful Hormones

Growth hormone helps all the parts of your body grow. Other hormones have jobs that help your body in different ways.

Sleep

Hungry

Angry

Happiness

Energy

Growth

Some hormones help you sleep better. Other hormones tell you when you are hungry.

BUMP BUMP

BUMP BUMP

BUMP BUMP

BUMP BUMP

One hormone makes your heart beat faster. This gives your body more energy to run away quickly from something scary.

Record Breakers

The shortest person who ever lived was Chandra Bahadur Dangi. He was 21 ½ inches (54 ½ cm) tall!

Robert Wadlow was the tallest man who ever lived. He was almost 9 feet (2 ¾ m) tall!

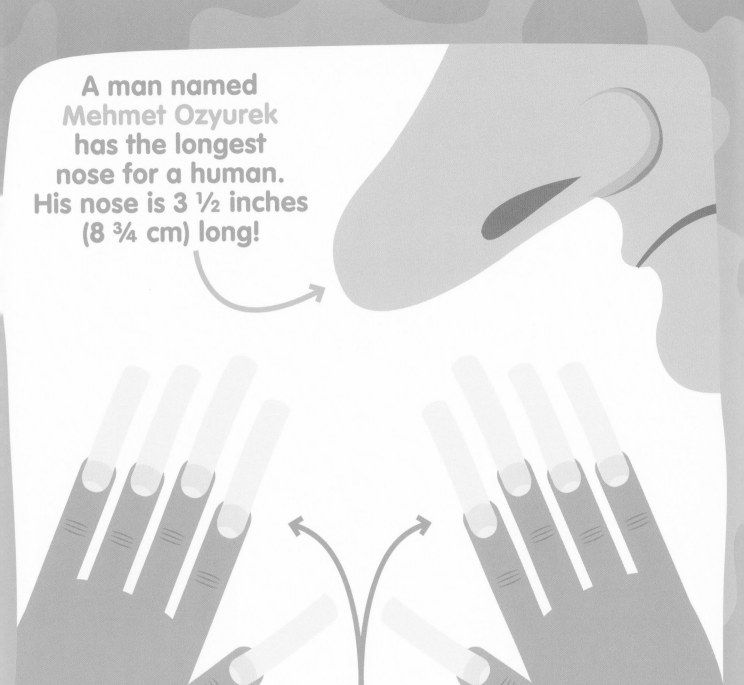

A man named **Mehmet Ozyurek** has the longest nose for a human. His nose is 3 ½ inches (8 ¾ cm) long!

The longest fingernails ever were almost 28 ½ feet (8 ¾ m) long!

Glossary

calcium   Natural substance used by the body to grow healthy bones and teeth

chemicals   Substances produced in the body, such as hormones

energy   The power to do work

glands   Parts of the body that produce substances, such as hormones

hormones   Chemicals in the body that give instructions to body parts, telling them what to do

nutrients   Substances that people need to grow and stay healthy

pace   The ongoing speed at which something moves

trim   To cut a little bit off something

Index